Benjamin Franklin on Immigration to America, Slavery,

and

Other Papers Descriptive of Early America

Benjamin Franklin on Immigration to America, Slavery,

and

Other Papers Descriptive of Early America

by BENJAMIN FRANKLIN

Introduction by Eric J. Miller

CONTENTS

INTRODUCTION

Reproduced here are eight short works by Benjamin Franklin that he wrote during the later years of his illustrious career. As such, they may be said to contain some of the wisdom that came from his remarkably long and productive life experience.

Benjamin Franklin was born in 1706 in Boston, which was then part of the British colony known as Massachusetts Bay. In fact, Franklin considered himself a Briton—and a loyal one—for much of his life until the revolution in the thirteen colonies made it clear that he was, indeed, an American.

Franklin's life spanned nearly the entire 18th century—the century of the Enlightenment and the American Revolution—two movements that he both personified and contributed mightily to. He died at the age of 84 in 1790 in Philadelphia, which was then fittingly serving as the capital city of the new United States of America that owed so much to him.

Among the Founding Fathers, George Washington stands alone as the "Father of his Country", and others such Thomas Jefferson and John Adams, no doubt, have greater name recognition in modern times, but it is Franklin who earned the title of "The First American" for both his role in founding the nation and for the manner in which he exemplified the emerging American character. Though generations of Americans growing up and going to school in the 20th century tended to learn about and view Franklin as either a kindly old man full of clever one-liners or as an eccentric inventor who half-wittingly flew a kite in a storm to discover electricity, the truth is profoundly more interesting. Throughout the Western world, Franklin was widely considered the greatest American of his day as well as in the decades following his death. It was not until the office of the President of the United States—a position that Franklin never held—came to occupy such a place of prominence that Franklin's star began to fade somewhat in the American psyche.

One hardly knows where to begin when attempting to describe who and what Benjamin Franklin was. He was a polymath—a true Renaissance man—whose talents and achievements spanned a stunning variety of fields. He was a philosopher, political theorist, statesman, and diplomat. He served as President of Pennsylvania, United States Minister to France, US Postmaster General, and he was a signer of both the Declaration of Independence and the Constitution. He was an inventor, scientist, author, and civic activist. His experiments with electricity are legendary; his mapping of the Gulf Stream revolutionized sailing; his ingenious discoveries and devices such as the lightning rod, Franklin stove, and bifocals won him universal praise, numerous honorary degrees, and a seat at the British Royal Society. His contributions to economics, meteorology, music, psychology, and education are less well known but have perhaps been equally significant in the advancement of human knowledge and well-being. He was an early pioneer in population studies, including slave demographics. He created one of the first volunteer firefighters groups. As an advocate of paper currency, he printed paper money with innovative anti-counterfeiting techniques he developed. He played and composed classical music, and Beethoven even wrote a sonata for an instrument—the armonica—that he created. He founded the American Philosophical Society and the school that would become the University of Pennsylvania. The list goes on and on. There was almost no limit to what the man could do.

He was, as H.W. Brands puts it in his prize-winning biography *The First American*, "quite simply one of the most illustrious scientists and thinkers on earth. ... The ablest minds of the age consulted him on matters large and small. Kings and emperors summoned him to court, where they admired his brilliance and basked in its reflected glory." Historian Walter Isaacson, in his biography of Franklin, is less colorful but equally emphatic that Franklin was "the most accomplished American of his age and the most influential in inventing the type of society America would become."

Today Benjamin Franklin is, appropriately, known and admired primarily for his political and scientific accomplishments. It was writing—and printing—

however, that afforded Franklin his first profession and the financial means to focus his time and talents on the things for which he is more acclaimed. Few realize how prolific Franklin was as a writer. The National Archives includes 13,947 works attributed to Franklin, ranging from his early days as a newspaper apprentice, to voluminous political and personal correspondence, to authoritative scientific treatises. The Digital Franklin Papers (freely available on the internet at www.franklinpapers.org) includes about twice that number. The sheer number and variety of his written work again demonstrates the true range of his genius.

Collected here in this short volume, *Benjamin Franklin on Immigration to America, Slavery, and Other Papers Descriptive of Early America*, are just eight of these works—short pieces written by Franklin during the last years of his life. The first three articles were written and first published around 1784 while Franklin was still in residence in France. The later four articles are among the last public statements Franklin made before his death in Philadelphia in 1790. Readers will notice some differences in English language conventions (vocabulary, spelling, and grammatical inflections, among others) used by Franklin. None of these are likely to cause serious misunderstanding, however, and the words of Franklin, as he wrote them, as reproduced here in their original form.

Franklin was nearly as well-known—and perhaps equally well-loved—in Europe as he was in the country of his birth. He spent almost two decades living in London—from the mid-1750s to mid-1770s—and another ten years after that in France. When Franklin first arrived in Paris in 1776 as America's first commissioner for the newly established United States, his presence was hailed by the French in an almost uncomprehending manner. Franklin wrote back to his daughter in Pennsylvania saying that "My picture is everywhere, on the lids of snuff boxes, on rings, busts. The numbers sold are incredible. My portrait is a best seller. Your father's face is now as well known as the man in the moon." Fellow diplomat John Adams— somewhat annoyed by the hysteria—wrote of Franklin: "His reputation is greater than that of Newton, Frederick the Great, or Voltaire; his character more revered than all of them."

During his years in France, Franklin resided outside Paris at Passy, where we set up a printing press and continued in the field that had launched him. It was here that the first three papers (*Information*, *Remarks*, and *State of America*) in this volume were written and first published when Franklin was in his late seventies. The middle article in this book (*Comparison*) is actually the earliest one written, appearing in 1777. It is included here as a complement to *State of America*, the two pieces showing both how Franklin saw the new nation at the time and also his vision for what he hoped it would become.

As part of his duties as the highest ranking American minister in Europe, he was continually burdened with inquiries from emigrants, or as he explained: "I am pestered continually with Numbers of Letters from People in different Parts of Europe, who would go to settle in America; but who manifest very extravagant Expectations, such as I can by no means encourage; and who appear otherwise to be very improper Persons. To save myself Trouble I have just printed some Copies of the enclosed little Piece, which I purpose to send hereafter in Answer to such Letters."

Information to Those Who Would Remove to America was one of several pamphlets printed by Franklin at Passy around 1784. These were translated and copies printed in both French and English. It is not known how many copies of *Information* Franklin printed, nor how many he may have left his successor, Thomas Jefferson. In 1788, however, having no more copies of what he described as that "petite brochure de M. Franklin" to give to prospective emigrants, Jefferson commissioned new ones. Without a private press at his disposal like Franklin, however, he was obliged to pay for the reprints.

For many years, the pamphlet served to correct common misconceptions about North America, to provide a foundation to what the new nation stood for, and to encourage hard-working Europeans seeking opportunities to emigrate to a land where industry was rewarded above title and real liberty and tolerance were afforded to all classes.

As can be expected from a man well beyond the average life expectancy of his era, Franklin's years in France were occasionally marked by ill health—mostly due to painful gout and bladder stones. During these times, often confined to his home, he spent considerable time reflecting on the differences among peoples and nations, considering how to characterize the nation he had helped to create. He wrote several pieces contrasting the New World—or what he wanted America to be—with the culture of Old World.

Remarks Concerning the Savages of North America is in some ways the most surprising of the pamphlets Franklin printed at Passy. Whereas his purposes in distributing *Information* and *Comparison* are clear, his own autobiography is silent as to *Remarks*. It may have been an attempt to neutralize stories of Indian savagery that were deterring potential emigrants from settling the American frontier, as he was often advocating in his role as ambassador. Perhaps it is merely an expression of Franklin's firsthand observations of Indian tribes and his appreciation for their lifestyle. Satirical as he often was, however, *Remarks* seems also to be calling out the narrow-mindedness and hypocrisy of most European nations when viewing those different from themselves.

The Internal State of America and *Comparison of Great Britain and America* illustrate Franklin's confidence in the virtues of the United States. Though he certainly understood the perils and uncertainties facing the new nation, his personal correspondence along with papers such as these demonstrate Franklin's desire to defend against rumors and reports of post-revolutionary troubles in America. England, naturally, was all too eager to believe that the new nation would fail, and other nations in Europe were often equally skeptical about the success or survival of the new nation. *State of America* and *Comparison* were largely attempts by Franklin to rebut such points of view and, in the case of *Comparison*, to encourage European support throughout the War of Independence.

In all of these papers, Franklin's faith in the American character and his optimism in the future prospects of the United States shine through. A sentiment that he repeated frequently was that only a virtuous people are capable of freedom.

Franklin returned to the United States in 1785. He was nearly eighty years old. After George Washington, he certainly was the most revered and respected leader in the new nation. He was duly elected president of Pennsylvania and also chosen to attend the convention in Philadelphia that would become known as the Constitutional Convention. Only Washington and Franklin were given any serious consideration for president of the convention. Franklin quickly deferred to Washington largely out of concern for his age and health, but also because he understood that Washington's leadership was paramount to the convention's success.

Though he rarely spoke up during the proceedings, Franklin's contributions were evident, especially regarding the grand compromise that created the two-house Congress with proportional representation in the House of Representatives and equal representation among the states in the Senate.

On the last day of the convention, Franklin wanted to give a short speech prior to the signing of the final draft that would become the new constitution. As had been his custom during most of the convention, however,

Franklin felt to weak to deliver the speech himself. It was read by fellow Pennsylvania delegate James Wilson. Franklin then moved that the convention adopt the final draft. The motion was adopted.

Not all of Franklin's ideas were popular or accepted by his fellow delegates. He had suggested, for example, that the executive under the new constitution receive no compensation beyond expenses. As demonstrated in *Remarks*, his respect for Native Americans and his sincerity in dealing with them were also not often shared by other state and national leaders. His views on slavery, which he probably came to rather late in life, were perhaps among his most radical.

Slavery and indentured servitude were an accepted part of life in early colonial America. Almost all of the founding fathers owned slaves at one time or another, including Franklin himself. When he first went to England in 1757, he brought two household slaves with him, which he mentions only casually in his correspondence. By the time he returned to America in 1785, however, he seems clearly to have changed his feelings regarding the topic. He was convinced that not only the slave trade should be eliminated, but that all slavery should be abolished everywhere.

The final three papers here reveal Franklin's thinking on abolitionism. In April 1787, he was elected president of a Pennsylvania Society for Promoting the Abolition of Slavery, and much of his correspondence during the remainder of his life was devoted to this subject. In late 1789, the society issued *An Address to the Public* introducing their platform and efforts, which also included a carefully considered program of the education for free blacks.

The following February, the society sent a *Petition* to the new United States Congress under the Constitution for a federal prohibition of slavery. When Congress declined to hear the petition, Franklin responded in vintage form, penning a satirical *Letter to the Editor of the Federal Gazette on the Slave Trade* under the pseudonym Historicus. Quoting one Sidi Mehemet Ibrahim, a member of the Algerian governing council, he gave the arguments against a supposed petition for granting freedom to Christians held in slavery in Africa. They were, of course, the same arguments used by the United States Congress against the petition presented by Franklin's abolition society.

Since his earliest days as a writer when he anonymously penned the brilliant Silence Dogood letters as a teenager, Franklin had often written under pseudonyms. His most famous pen name, no doubt, was Richard Saunders of *Poor Richard's Almanack*—the publication that greatly helped to establish Franklin's fame and also gave him his financial independence. It is fitting that his very last known public statement was a cunning satire on slavery in America, also written under a nom de plume. He died less than a month after its publication on April 17, 1790.

Here, then, are eight of Benjamin Franklin's final papers. Far from being the words of a worn-out man facing a decline in his mental capabilities, they reveal Franklin at his finest with his views on morality and his vision for an ideal society at their fullest maturity.

Fellow Founding Father Benjamin Rush commented that Franklin in his final years was "as cheerful and gay as a young man of five-and-twenty, his conversation was full of the wisdom and experience of mellow old age, the evening of his life was marked by the same activity of his moral and intellectual powers which distinguished its meridian."

To the end of his life, Franklin maintained an optimistic view toward human nature. The goodness he saw in mankind was no different in Negroes and native Americans than it was in white Americans and Caucasians; he believed his fellow scientists and politicians to be no better than common farmers and tradesmen. He lived and died as a truly virtuous citizen, as close as any to achieving the full potential of the human spirit. As such, his ideas and words are still relevant and needed in a world still very much striving to secure the rights to life, liberty, and the pursuit of happiness for all people.

Benjamin Franklin on Immigration to America, Slavery,

and

Other Papers Descriptive of Early America

By BENJAMIN FRANKLIN

1.

Information to Those Who Would Remove to America

circa 1784

Many persons in Europe having directly or by letters, expressed to the writer of this, who is well acquainted with North-America, their desire of transporting and establishing themselves in that country; but who appear to him to have formed, through ignorance, mistaken ideas and expectations of what is to be obtained there; he thinks it may be useful, and prevent inconvenient, expensive, and fruitless removals and voyages of improper persons, if he gives some clearer and truer notions of that part of the world, than appear to have hitherto prevailed.

He finds it is imagined by numbers, that the inhabitants of North America are rich, capable of rewarding, and disposed to reward, all sorts of ingenuity; that they are at the same time ignorant of all the sciences, and consequently, that strangers, possessing talents in the belles-lettres, fine arts, &c.

must be highly esteemed, and so well paid, as to become easily rich themselves; that there are also abundance of profitable offices to be disposed of, which the natives are not qualified to fill; and that, having few persons of family among them, strangers of birth must be greatly respected, and of course easily obtain the best of those offices, which will make all their fortunes: that the governments too, to encourage emigrations from Europe, not only pay the expence of personal transportation, but give lands gratis to strangers, with negroes to work for them, utensils of husbandry, and stocks of cattle. These are all wild imaginations; and those who go to America with expectations founded upon them will surely find themselves disappointed.

The truth is, that though there are in that country few people so miserable as the poor of Europe, there are also very few that in Europe would be called rich; it is rather a general happy mediocrity that prevails. There are few great proprietors of the soil, and few tenants; most people cultivate their own lands, or follow some handicraft or merchandise; very few rich enough to live idly upon their rents or incomes, or to pay the high prices given in Europe for painting, statues, architecture, and the other works of art, that are more curious than useful. Hence the natural geniuses, that have arisen in America with such talents, have uniformly quitted that country for Europe, where they can be more suitably rewarded. It is true, that letters and mathematical knowledge are in esteem there, but they are at the same time more common than is apprehended; there being already existing nine colleges or universities, viz. four in New England, and one in each of the provinces of New York, New Jersey, Pennsylvania, Maryland, and

Virginia, all furnished with learned professors; besides a number of smaller academies: these educate many of their youth in the languages, and those sciences that qualify men for the professions of divinity, law, or physic. Strangers indeed are by no means excluded from exercising those professions; and the quick increase of inhabitants every where gives them a chance of employ, which they have in common with the natives. Of civil offices, or employments, there are few; no superfluous ones, as in Europe; and it is a rule established in some of the states, that no office should be so profitable as to make it desirable. The thirty-sixth article of the constitution of Pennsylvania runs expressly in these words: "As every freeman, to preserve his independence (if he has not a sufficient estate) ought to have some profession, calling, trade, or farm, whereby he may honestly subsist, there can be no necessity for, nor use in, establishing offices of profit; the usual effects of which are dependence and servility, unbecoming freemen, in the possessors and expectants; faction, contention, corruption, and disorder among the people. Wherefore, whenever an office, through increase of fees or otherwise, becomes so profitable, as to occasion many to apply for it, the profits ought to be lessened by the legislature."

These ideas prevailing more or less in all the United States, it cannot be worth any man's while, who has a means of living at home, to expatriate himself, in hopes of obtaining a profitable civil office in America; and as to military offices, they are at an end with the war, the armies being disbanded. Much less is it adviseable for a person to go thither, who has no other quality to recommend him but his birth. In Europe it has indeed its value; but it is a commodity that cannot be carried to a worse market than to that of America, where people do not enquire concerning a stranger, *What is he?* but *What can he do?* If he has any useful art, he is welcome; and if he exercises it, and behaves well, he will be respected by all that know him; but a mere man of quality, who on that account wants to live upon the public by some office or salary, will be despised and disregarded. The husbandman is in honour there, and even the mechanic, because their employments are useful. The people have a saying, that God Almighty is himself a mechanic, the greatest in the universe; and he is respected and admired more for the variety, ingenuity, and utility of his handiworks, than for the antiquity of his family. They are pleased with the observation of a negro, and frequently mention it, that Boccarora (meaning the white man) make de black man workee, make de horse workee, make de ox workee, make ebery ting workee; only de hog. He de hog, no workee; he eat, he drink, he walk about, he go to sleep when he please, he libb like a gentleman. According to these opinions of the Americans, one of them would think himself more obliged to a genealogist, who could prove for him that his ancestors and relations for ten generations had been ploughmen, smiths, carpenters, turners, weavers, tanners, or even shoemakers, and consequently that they were useful members of society; than if he could only prove that they were gentlemen, doing nothing of value, but living idly on the labour of others, mere *fruges consumere nati*, and otherwise *good for nothing*, till by their death their estates, like the carcase of the negro's gentleman-hog, come to be *cut up*.

4

With regard to encouragements for strangers from government, they are really only what are derived from good laws and liberty. Strangers are welcome, because there is room enough for them all, and therefore the old inhabitants are not jealous of them; the laws protect them sufficiently, so that they have no need of the patronage of great men; and every one will enjoy securely the profits of his industry. But if he does not bring a fortune with him, he must work and be industrious to live. One or two years residence give him all the rights of a citizen; but the government does not at present, whatever it may have done in former times, hire people to become settlers, by paying their passages, giving land, negroes, utensils, stock, or any other kind of emolument whatsoever. In short, America is the land of labour, and by no means what the English call Lubberland, and the French Pays de Cocagne, where the streets are said to be paved with half-peck loaves, the houses tiled with pancakes, and where the fowls fly about ready roasted, crying, *Come eat me!*

Who then are the kind of persons to whom an emigration to America may be advantageous? And what are the advantages they may reasonably expect?

Land being cheap in that country, from the vast forests still void of inhabitants, and not likely to be occupied in an age to come, insomuch that the propriety of an hundred acres of fertile soil full of wood may be obtained near the frontiers, in many places, for eight or ten guineas, hearty young labouring men, who understand the husbandry of corn and cattle, which is nearly the same in that country as in Europe, may easily establish themselves there. A little money saved of the good wages they receive there, while they work for others, enables them to buy the land and begin their plantation, in which they are assisted by the good-will of their neighbours, and some credit. Multitudes of poor people from England, Ireland, Scotland, and Germany, have by this means in a few years become wealthy farmers, who, in their own countries, where all the lands are fully occupied, and the wages of labour low, could never have emerged from the mean condition wherein they were born.

From the salubrity of the air, the healthiness of the climate, the plenty of good provisions, and the encouragement to early marriages, by the certainty of subsistence in cultivating the earth, the increase of inhabitants by natural generation is very rapid in America, and becomes still more so by the accession of strangers; hence there is a continual demand for more artisans of all the necessary and useful kinds, to supply those cultivators of the earth with houses, and with furniture and utensils of the grosser sorts, which cannot so well be brought from Europe. Tolerably good workmen in any of those mechanic arts are sure to find employ, and to be well paid for their work, there being no restraints preventing strangers from exercising any art they understand, nor any permission necessary. If they are poor, they begin first as servants or journeymen; and if they are sober, industrious, and frugal, they soon become masters, establish themselves in business, marry, raise families, and become respectable citizens.

Also, persons of moderate fortunes and capitals, who, having a number of children to provide for, are desirous of bringing them up to industry, and to secure estates for their posterity, have opportunities of doing it in America, which Europe does not afford. There they may be taught and practise profitable mechanic arts, without incurring disgrace on that account, but on the contrary acquiring respect by such abilities. There small capitals laid out in lands, which daily become more valuable by the increase of people, afford a solid prospect of ample fortunes thereafter for those children. The writer of this has known several instances of large tracts of land, bought, on what was then the frontier of Pennsylvania, for ten pounds per hundred acres, which, when the settlements had been extended far beyond them, sold readily, without any improvement made upon them, for three pounds per acre. The acre in America is the same with the English acre, or the acre of Normandy.

Those, who desire to understand the state of government in America, would do well to read the constitutions of the several states, and the articles of confederation that bind the whole together for general purposes, under the direction of one assembly, called the congress. These constitutions have been printed, by order of congress, in America; two editions of them have also been printed in London; and a good translation of them into French has lately been published at Paris.

Several of the princes of Europe of late, from an opinion of advantage to arise by producing all commodities and manufactures within their own dominions, so as to diminish or render useless their importations, have endeavoured to entice workmen from other countries, by high salaries, privileges, &c. Many persons, pretending to be skilled in various great manufactures, imagining, that America must be in want of them, and that the congress would probably be disposed to imitate the princes above mentioned, have proposed to go over, on condition of having their passages paid, lands given, salaries appointed, exclusive privileges for terms of years, &c. Such persons, on reading the articles of confederation, will find, that the congress have no power committed to them, or money put into their hands, for such purposes; and that if any such encouragement is given, it must be by the government of some separate state. This, however, has rarely been done in America; and when it has been done, it has rarely succeeded, so as to establish a manufacture, which the country was not yet so ripe for as to encourage private persons to set it up; labour being generally too dear there, and hands difficult to be kept together, every one desiring to be a master, and the cheapness of land inclining many to leave trades for agriculture. Some indeed have met with success, and are carried on to advantage; but they are generally such as require only a few hands, or wherein great part of the work is performed by machines. Goods that are bulky, and of so small value as not well to bear the expence of freight, may often be made cheaper in the country than they can be imported; and the manufacture of such goods will be profitable wherever there is a sufficient demand. The farmers in America produce indeed a good deal of wool and flax; and none is exported, it is all worked up; but it is in the way of domestic manufacture, for the use of the family. The buying up quantities of wool and flax, with the design to employ spinners, weavers, &c. and form great establishments, producing quantities of linen and woollen goods for sale, has been several times attempted in different provinces; but those projects have generally failed, goods of equal value being imported cheaper. And when the governments have been solicited to support such schemes by encouragements, in money, or by imposing duties on importation of such goods, it has been generally refused, on this principle, that if the country is ripe for the manufacture, it may be carried on by private persons to advantage; and if not, it is a folly to think of forcing nature. Great establishments of manufacture require great numbers of poor to do the work for small wages; those poor are to be found in Europe, but will not be found in America, till the lands are all taken up and cultivated, and the excess of people, who cannot get land, want employment. The manufacture of silk, they say, is natural in France, as that of cloth in England, because each country produces in plenty the first material: but if England will have a manufacture of silk as well as that of cloth, and France of cloth as well as that of silk, these unnatural operations must be supported by mutual prohibitions, or high duties on the importation of each other's goods; by which means the workmen are enabled to tax the home consumer by greater prices, while the higher wages they receive makes them neither happier nor richer, since they only drink more and work less. Therefore the governments in America do nothing to encourage such projects. The people, by this means, are not imposed on either by the merchant or mechanic: if the merchant demands too much profit on imported shoes, they buy of the shoe-maker; and if he asks too high a price, they take them of the merchant: thus the two professions are checks on each other. The shoemaker, however, has, on the whole, a considerable profit upon his labour in America, beyond what he had in Europe, as he can add to his price a sum nearly equal to all the expences of freight and commission, risque or insurance, &c. necessarily charged by the merchant. And the case is the same with the workmen in every other mechanic art. Hence it is, that artisans generally live better and more easily in America than in Europe; and such as are good economists make a comfortable provision for age, and for their children. Such may, therefore, remove with advantage to America.

In the old long-settled countries of Europe, all arts, trades, professions, farms, &c. are so full, that it is difficult for a poor man who has children to place them where they may gain, or learn to gain, a decent livelihood. The artisans, who fear creating future rivals in business, refuse to take apprentices, but upon conditions of money, maintenance, or the like, which the parents are unable to comply with. Hence the youth are dragged up in ignorance of every gainful art, and obliged to become soldiers, or servants, or thieves, for a subsistence. In America, the rapid increase of inhabitants takes away that fear of rivalship, and artisans willingly receive apprentices from the hope of profit by their labour, during the remainder of the time stipulated, after they shall be instructed. Hence it is easy for poor families to get their children instructed; for the artisans are so desirous of apprentices, that many of them will even give money to the parents, to have boys from ten to fifteen years of age bound apprentices to them, till the age of twenty-one; and many poor parents have, by that means, on their arrival in the country, raised money enough to buy land sufficient to establish themselves, and to subsist the rest of their family by agriculture. These contracts for apprentices are made before a magistrate, who regulates the agreement according to reason and justice, and, having in view the formation of a future useful citizen, obliges the master to engage by a written indenture, not only that, during the time of service stipulated, the apprentice shall be duly provided with meat, drink, apparel, washing, and lodging, and at its expiration with a complete new suit of clothes, but also, that he shall be taught to read, write, and cast accounts; and that he shall be well instructed in the art or profession of his master, or some other, by which he may afterwards gain a livelihood, and be able in his turn to raise a family. A copy of this indenture is given to the apprentice or his friends, and the magistrate keeps a record of it, to which recourse may be had, in case of failure by the master in any point of performance. This desire among the masters, to have more hands employed in working for them, induces them to pay the passages of young persons, of both sexes, who, on their arrival, agree to serve them one, two, three, or four years; those who have already learned a trade, agreeing for a shorter term, in proportion to their skill, and the consequent immediate value of their service; and those who have none, agreeing for a longer term, in consideration of being taught an art their poverty would not permit them to acquire in their own country.

The almost general mediocrity of fortune that prevails in America, obliging its people to follow some business for subsistence, those vices, that arise usually from idleness, are in a great measure prevented. Industry and constant employment are great preservatives of the morals and virtue of a nation. Hence bad examples to youth are more rare in America, which must be a comfortable consideration to parents. To this may be truly added, that serious religion, under its various denominations, is not only tolerated, but respected and practised. Atheism is unknown there; infidelity rare and secret; so that persons may live to a great age in that country, without having their piety shocked by meeting with either an atheist or an infidel. And the Divine Being seems to have manifested his approbation of the mutual forbearance and kindness with which the different sects treat each other, by the remarkable prosperity with which he has been pleased to favour the whole country.

2.

Remarks Concerning the Savages of North America

circa 1784

Savages we call them, because their manners differ from ours, which we think the perfection of civility; they think the same of theirs.

Perhaps, if we could examine the manners of different nations with impartiality, we should find no people so rude, as to be without any rules of politeness; nor any so polite, as not to have some remains of rudeness.

The Indian men, when young, are hunters and warriors; when old, counsellors; for all their government is by the council or advice of the sages; there is no force, there are no prisons, no officers to compel obedience, or inflict punishment. Hence they generally study oratory, the best speaker having the most influence. The Indian women till the ground, dress the food, nurse and bring up the children, and preserve and hand down to posterity the memory of public transactions. These employments of men and women are accounted natural and honourable. Having few artificial wants, they have abundance of leisure for improvement by conversation. Our laborious manner of life, compared with theirs, they esteem slavish and base; and the learning on which we value ourselves, they regard as frivolous and useless. An instance of this occurred at the treaty of Lancaster, in Pennsylvania, anno 1744, between the government of Virginia and the six nations. After the principal business was settled, the commissioners from Virginia acquainted the Indians by a speech, that there was at Williamsburg a college, with a fund, for educating Indian youth; and that if the chiefs of the Six Nations would send down half a dozen of their sons to that college, the government would take care that they should be well provided for, and instructed in all the learning of the white people. It is one of the Indian rules of politeness, not to answer a public proposition the same day that it is made; they think it would be treating it as a light matter, and that they show it respect by taking time to consider it, as of a matter important. They therefore deferred their answer till the day following; when their speaker began, by expressing their deep sense of the kindness of the Virginia government, in making them that offer; "for we know," says he, "that you highly esteem the kind of learning taught in those colleges, and that the maintenance of our young men, while with you, would be very expensive to you. We are convinced therefore, that you mean to do us good by your proposal; and we thank you heartily. But you, who are wise, must know, that different nations have different conceptions of things; and you will therefore not take it amiss, if our ideas of this kind of education happen not to be the same with yours. We have had some experience of it: several of our young people were formerly brought up at the colleges of the northern provinces; they were instructed in all your sciences; but when they came back to us, they were bad runners, ignorant of every means of living in the woods, unable to bear either cold or hunger, knew neither how to build a cabin, take a deer, or kill an enemy, spoke our language imperfectly, were therefore neither fit for hunters, warriors, or counsellors; they were totally good for nothing. We are however not the less obliged by your kind offer, though we decline accepting it: and to show our grateful sense of it, if the gentlemen of Virginia will send us a dozen of their sons, we will take great care of their education, instruct them in all we know, and make *men* of them."

Having frequent occasions to hold public councils, they have acquired great order and decency in conducting them. The old men sit in the foremost ranks, the warriors in the next, and the women and children in the hindmost. The business of the women is to take exact notice of what passes, imprint it in their memories, for they have no writing, and communicate it to their children. They are the records of the council, and they preserve tradition of the stipulations in treaties a hundred years back; which, when we compare with our writings, we always find exact. He that would speak, rises. The rest observe a profound silence. When he has finished and sits down, they leave him five or six minutes to recollect, that, if he has omitted any thing he intended to say, or has any thing to add, he may rise again and deliver it. To interrupt another, even in common conversation, is reckoned highly indecent.

How different this is from the conduct of a polite British house of commons, where scarce a day passes without some confusion, that makes the speaker hoarse in calling *to order*; and how different from the mode of conversation in many polite companies of Europe, where, if you do not deliver your sentence with great rapidity, you are cut off in the middle of it by the impatient loquacity of those you converse with, and never suffered to finish it!

The politeness of these savages in conversation is indeed carried to excess, since it does not permit them to contradict or deny the truth of what is asserted in their presence. By this means they indeed avoid disputes; but then it becomes difficult to know their minds, or what impression you make upon them. The missionaries who have attempted to convert them to Christianity, all complain of this as one of the great difficulties of their mission. The Indians hear with patience the truths of the gospel explained to them, and give their usual tokens of assent and approbation: you would think they were convinced. No such matter. It is mere civility.

A Swedish minister, having assembled the chiefs of the Sasquehannah Indians, made a sermon to them, acquainting them with the principal historical facts on which our religion is founded; such as the fall of our first parents by eating an apple, the coming of Christ to repair the mischief, his miracles and suffering, &c.— When he had finished, an Indian orator stood up to thank him. "What you have told us," says he, "is all very good. It is indeed bad to eat apples. It is better to make them all into cyder. We are much obliged by your kindness in coming so far, to tell us those things which you have heard from your mothers. In return, I will tell you some of those we have heard from ours.

"In the beginning, our fathers had only the flesh of animals to subsist on, and if their hunting was unsuccessful, they were starving. Two of our young hunters having killed a deer, made a fire in the woods to broil some parts of it. When they were about to satisfy their hunger, they beheld a beautiful young woman descend from the clouds, and seat herself on that hill which you see yonder among the Blue Mountains. They said to each other, it is a spirit that perhaps has smelt our broiling venison, and wishes to eat of it: let us offer some to her. They presented her with the tongue: she was pleased with the taste of it, and said, Your kindness shall be rewarded. Come to this place after thirteen moons, and you shall find something that will be of great benefit in nourishing you and your children to the latest generations. They did so, and to their surprise, found plants they had never seen before; but which, from that ancient time, have been constantly cultivated among us, to our great advantage. Where her right hand had touched the ground, they found maize; where her left hand had touched it, they found kidney-beans; and where her backside had sat on it, they found tobacco." The good missionary, disgusted with this idle tale, said, "What I delivered to you were sacred truths, but what you tell me is mere fable, fiction, and falsehood." The Indian, offended, replied, "My brother, it seems your friends have not done you justice in your education; they have not well instructed you in the rules of common civility. You saw that we, who understand and

17

practice those rules, believed all your stories, why do you refuse to believe ours?"

When any of them come into our towns, our people are apt to crowd round them, gaze upon them, and incommode them where they desire to be private; this they esteem great rudeness, and the effect of the want of instruction in the rules of civility and good manners. "We have," say they, "as much curiosity as you, and when you come into our towns, we wish for opportunities of looking at you; but for this purpose we hide ourselves behind bushes, where you are to pass, and never intrude ourselves into your company."

Their manner of entering one another's villages has likewise its rules. It is reckoned uncivil in travelling strangers, to enter a village abruptly, without giving notice of their approach. Therefore, as soon as they arrive within hearing, they stop and hollow, remaining there till invited to enter. Two old men usually come out to them, and lead them in. There is in every village a vacant dwelling, called the strangers' house. Here they are placed, while the old men go round from hut to hut, acquainting the inhabitants, that strangers are arrived, who are probably hungry and weary; and every one sends them what he can spare of victuals, and skins to repose on. When the strangers are refreshed, pipes and tobacco are brought; and then, but not before, conversation begins, with enquiries who they are, whither bound, what news, &c. and it usually ends with offers of service, if the strangers have occasion for guides, or any necessaries for continuing their journey; and nothing is exacted for the entertainment.

The same hospitality, esteemed among them as a principal virtue, is practised by private persons; of which *Conrad Weiser*, our interpreter, gave me the following instance. He had been naturalized among the Six Nations, and spoke well the Mohuck language. In going through the Indian country, to carry a message from our governor to the council at Onondaga, he called at the habitation of Canassetego, an old acquaintance, who embraced him, spread furs for him to sit on, and placed before him some boiled beans and venison, and mixed some rum and water for his drink. When he was well refreshed, and had lit his pipe, Canassetego began to converse with him: asked how he had fared the many years since they had seen each other, whence he then came, what occasioned the journey, &c. Conrad answered all his questions; and when the discourse began to flag, the Indian, to continue it, said, "Conrad, you have lived long among the white people, and know something of their customs; I have been sometimes at Albany, and have observed, that once in seven days they shut up their shops, and assemble all in the great house; tell me what it is for? What do they do there?" "They meet there," says Conrad, "to hear and learn *good things*." "I do not doubt," says the Indian, "that they tell you so; they have told me the same: but I doubt the truth of what they say, and I will tell you my reasons. I went lately to Albany to sell my skins and buy blankets, knives, powder, rum, &c. You know I used generally to deal with Hans Hanson; but I was a little inclined this time to try some other merchants. However, I called first upon Hans, and asked him what he would give for beaver. He said he could not give more than four shillings a pound: but, says he, I cannot talk on business now; this is the day when we meet together to learn *good things*, and I am going to the meeting. So I thought to myself, since I cannot do any business to-day, I may as well go to the meeting too, and I went with him. There stood up a man in black, and began to talk to the people very angrily. I did not understand what he said; but perceiving that he looked much at me, and at Hanson, I imagined he was angry at seeing me there; so I went out, sat down near the house, struck fire, and lit my pipe, waiting till the meeting should break up. I thought too, that the man had mentioned something of beaver, and I suspected it might be the subject of their meeting. So when they came out I accosted my merchant. Well, Hans, says I, I hope you have agreed to give more than four shillings a pound? No, says he, I cannot give so much, I cannot give more than three shillings and sixpence. I then spoke to several other dealers, but they all sung the same song, three and sixpence, three and sixpence. This made it clear to me that my suspicion was right; and that whatever they pretended of meeting to learn *good things*, the real purpose was to consult how to cheat Indians in the price of beaver. Consider but a little, Conrad, and you must be of my opinion. If they met so often to learn *good things*, they would certainly have learned some before this time. But they are still ignorant. You know our practice. If a white man, in travelling through our country, enters one of our cabins, we all treat him as I do you; we dry him if he is wet, we warm him if he is cold, and give him meat and drink, that he may allay his thirst and hunger; and we spread soft furs for him to rest and sleep on: we demand nothing in return. But if I go into a white man's house at

Albany, and ask for victuals and drink, they say, Where is your money? and if I have none, they say, Get out you Indian dog. You see they have not yet learned those little *good things*, that we need no meetings to be instructed in, because our mothers taught them to us when we were children; and therefore it is impossible their meetings should be, as they say, for any such purpose, or have any such effect; they are only to contrive *the cheating of Indians in the price of beaver*."

3.

The Internal State of America; Being a True Description of the Interest and Policy of That Vast Continent

circa 1784

There is a tradition, that, in the planting of New-England, the first settlers met with many difficulties and hardships; as is generally the case when a civilized people attempt establishing themselves in a wilderness country. Being piously disposed, they sought relief from Heaven, by laying their wants and distresses before the Lord, in frequent set days of fasting and prayer. Constant meditation and discourse on these subjects kept their minds gloomy and discontented; and, like the children of Israel, there were many disposed to return to that Egypt, which persecution had induced them to abandon. At length, when it was proposed in the assembly to proclaim another fast, a farmer of plain sense rose, and remarked, that the inconveniences they suffered, and concerning which they had so often wearied heaven with their complaints, were not so great as they might have expected, and were diminishing every day as the colony strengthened; that the earth began to reward their labour, and to furnish liberally for their subsistence; that the seas and rivers were found full of fish, the air sweet, the climate healthy; and, above all, that they were there in the full enjoyment of liberty, civil and religious: he therefore thought, that reflecting and conversing on these subjects would be more comfortable, as tending more to make them contented with their situation; and that it would be more becoming the gratitude they owed to the Divine Being, if, instead of a fast, they should proclaim a thanksgiving. His advice was taken; and from that day to this they have, in every year, observed circumstances of public felicity sufficient to furnish employment for a thanksgiving day; which is therefore constantly ordered and religiously observed.

I see in the public newspapers of different states frequent complaints of *hard times, deadness of trade, scarcity of money, &c. &c.* It is not my intention to assert or maintain, that these complaints are entirely without foundation. There can be no country or nation existing, in which there will not be some people so circumstanced, as to find it hard to gain a livelihood; people who are not in the way of any profitable trade, and with whom money is scarce, because they have nothing to give in exchange for it; and it is always in the power of a small number to make a great clamour. But let us take a cool view of the general state of our affairs, and perhaps the prospect will appear less gloomy than has been imagined.

The great business of the continent is agriculture. For one artisan, or merchant, I suppose, we have at least one hundred farmers, by far the greatest part cultivators of their own fertile lands, from whence many of them draw not only food necessary for their subsistence, but the materials of their clothing, so as to need very few foreign supplies; while they have a surplus of productions to dispose of, whereby wealth is gradually accumulated. Such has been the goodness of Divine Providence to these regions, and so favourable the climate, that, since the three or four years of hardship in the first settlement of our fathers here, a famine or scarcity has never been heard of amongst us; on the contrary, though some years may have been more, and others less plentiful, there has always been provision enough for ourselves, and a quantity to spare for exportation. And although the crops of last year were generally good, never was the farmer better paid for the part he can spare commerce, as the published price currents abundantly testify. The lands he possesses are also continually rising in value with the increase of population; and, on the whole, he is enabled to give such good wages to those who work for him, that all who are acquainted with the old world must agree, that in no part of it are the labouring poor so generally well fed, well clothed, well lodged, and well paid, as in the United States of America.

If we enter the cities, we find, that, since the revolution, the owners of houses and lots of ground have had their interest vastly augmented in value; rents have risen to an astonishing height, and thence encouragement to increase building, which gives employment to an abundance of workmen, as does also the increased luxury and splendour of living of the inhabitants, thus made richer. These workmen all demand and obtain much higher wages than any other part of the world would afford them, and are paid in ready money. This rank of people therefore do not, or ought not, to complain of hard times; and they make a very considerable part of the city inhabitants.

At the distance I live from our American fisheries, I cannot speak of them with any degree of certainty; but I have not heard, that the labour of the valuable race of men employed in them is worse paid, or that they meet with less success, than before the revolution. The whale-men indeed have been deprived of one market for their oil; but another, I hear, is opening for them, which it is hoped may be equally advantageous; and the demand is constantly increasing for their spermaceti candles, which therefore bear a much higher price than formerly.

There remain the merchants and shopkeepers. Of these, though they make but a small part of the whole nation, the number is considerable, too great indeed for the business they are employed in; for the consumption of goods in every country has its limits; the faculties of the people, that is, their ability to buy and pay, being equal only to a certain quantity of merchandize. If merchants calculate amiss on this proportion, and import too much, they will of course find the sale dull for the overplus, and some of them will say, that trade languishes. They should, and doubtless will, grow wiser by experience, and import less. If too many artificers in town, and farmers from the country, flattering themselves with the idea of leading easier lives, turn shopkeepers, the whole natural quantity of that business divided among them all may afford too small a share for each, and occasion complaints, that trading is dead; these may also suppose, that it is owing to scarcity of money, while, in fact, it is not so much from the fewness of buyers, as from the excessive number of sellers, that the mischief arises; and, if every shopkeeping farmer and mechanic would return to the use of his plough and working tools, there would remain of widows, and other women, shopkeepers sufficient for the business, which might then afford them a comfortable maintenance.

Whoever has travelled through the various parts of Europe, and observed how small is the proportion of people in affluence or easy circumstances there, compared with those in poverty and misery; the few rich and haughty landlords, the multitude of poor, abject, rack-rented, tythe-paying tenants, and half-paid and half-starved ragged labourers; and views here the happy mediocrity, that so generally prevails throughout these states, where the cultivator works for himself, and supports his family in decent plenty, will, methinks, see abundant reason to bless Divine Providence for the evident and great difference in our favour, and be convinced, that no nation known to us enjoys a greater share of human felicity.

It is true, that in some of the states there are parties and discords; but let us look back, and ask if we were ever without them? Such will exist wherever there is liberty; and perhaps they help to preserve it. By the collision of different sentiments, sparks of truth are struck out, and political light is obtained. The different factions, which at present divide us, aim all at the public good: the differences are only about the various modes of promoting it. Things, actions, measures, and objects of all kinds, present themselves to the minds of men in such a variety of lights, that it is not possible we should all think alike at the same time on every subject, when hardly the same man retains at all times the same ideas of it. Parties are therefore the common lot of humanity; and ours are by no means more mischievous or less beneficial than those of other countries, nations, and ages, enjoying in the same degree the great blessing of political liberty.

Some indeed among us are not so much grieved for the present state of our affairs, as apprehensive for the future. The growth of luxury alarms them, and they think we are from that alone in the high road to ruin. They observe, that no revenue is sufficient without economy, and that the most plentiful income of a whole people from the natural productions of their country may be dissipated in vain and needless expences, and poverty be introduced in the place of affluence. This may be possible. It however rarely happens: for there seems to be in every nation a greater proportion of industry and frugality, which tend to enrich, than of idleness and prodigality, which occasion poverty; so that upon the whole there is a continual accumulation. Reflect what Spain, Gaul, Germany, and Britain were in the time of the Romans, inhabited by people little richer than our savages, and consider the wealth they at present possess, in numerous well-built cities, improved farms, rich moveables, magazines stocked with valuable manufactures, to say nothing of plate jewels, and coined money; and all this, notwithstanding their bad, wasteful, plundering governments, and their mad destructive wars; and yet luxury and extravagant living has never suffered much restraint in those countries. Then consider the great proportion of industrious frugal farmers inhabiting the interior parts of these American states, and of whom the body of our nation consists, and judge whether it is possible, that the luxury of our sea-ports can be sufficient to ruin such a country.—If the importation of foreign luxuries could ruin a people, we should probably have been ruined long ago; for the British nation claimed a right, and practised it, of importing among us not only the superfluities of their own production, but those of every nation under heaven; we bought and consumed them, and yet we flourished and grew rich. At present our independent governments may do what we could not then do, discourage by heavy duties, or prevent by heavy prohibitions, such importations, and thereby grow richer; if, indeed, which may admit of dispute, the desire of adorning ourselves with fine clothes, possessing fine furniture, with elegant houses, &c. is not, by strongly inciting to labour and industry, the occasion of producing a greater value, than is consumed in the gratification of that desire.

The agriculture and fisheries of the United States are the great sources of our increasing wealth. He that puts a seed into the earth is recompensed, perhaps, by receiving forty out of it; and he who draws a fish out of our water, draws up a piece of silver.

Let us (and there is no doubt but we shall) be attentive to these, and then the power of rivals, with all their restraining and prohibiting acts, cannot much hurt us. We are sons of the earth and seas, and, like Antæus in the fable, if, in wrestling with a Hercules, we now and then receive a fall, the touch of our parents will communicate to us fresh strength and vigour to renew the contest.

4.

Comparison of Great Britain and America as to Credit

1777

In borrowing money a man's credit depends on some or all of the following particulars.

First, His known conduct respecting former loans, and his punctuality in discharging them.

Secondly, His industry.

Thirdly, His frugality.

Fourthly, The amount and the certainty of his income, and the freedom of his estate from the incumbrances of prior debts.

Fifthly, His well founded prospects of greater future ability, by the improvement of his estate in value, and by aids from others.

Sixthly, His known prudence in managing his general affairs, and the advantage they will probably receive from the loan which he desires.

Seventhly, His known probity and honest character, manifested by his voluntary discharge of debts, which he could not have been legally compelled to pay. The circumstances which give credit to an *individual* ought to have, and will have, their weight upon the lenders of money to *public bodies* or nations. If then we consider and compare Britain and America, in these several particulars, upon the question, "To which is it safest to lend money?" We shall find,

1. Respecting *former loans*, that America, which borrowed ten millions during the last war for the maintenance of her army of 25,000 men and other charges, had faithfully discharged and paid that debt, and all her other debts, in 1772. Whereas Britain, during those ten years of peace and profitable commerce, had made little or no reduction of her debt; but on the contrary, from time to time, diminished the hopes of her creditors, by a wanton diversion and misapplication of the sinking fund destined for discharging it.

2. Respecting *industry*; every man [in America] is employed, the greater part in cultivating their own lands, the rest in handicrafts, navigation, and commerce. An idle man there is a rarity, idleness and inutility are disgraceful. In England, the number of that character is immense, fashion has spread it far and wide; hence the embarrassments of private fortunes, and the daily bankruptcies arising from an universal fondness for appearance and expensive pleasures; and hence, in some degree, the mismanagement of public business; for habits of business, and ability in it, are acquired

only by practice; and where universal dissipation, and the perpetual pursuit of amusement are the mode, the youth, educated in it, can rarely afterwards acquire that patient attention and close application to affairs, which are so necessary to a statesman charged with the care of national welfare. *Hence* their frequent errors in policy, and hence the weariness at public councils, and backwardness in going to them, the constant unwillingness to engage in any measure that requires thought and consideration, and the readiness for postponing every new proposition; which postponing is therefore the only part of business that they come to be expert in, an expertness produced necessarily by so much daily practice. Whereas in America, men bred to close employment in their private affairs, attend with ease to those of the public, when engaged in them, and nothing fails through negligence.

3. Respecting *frugality*; the manner of living in America is more simple and less expensive than that in England: plain tables, plain clothing, and plain furniture in houses prevail, with few carriages of pleasure; there, an expensive appearance hurts credit, and is avoided: in England, it is often assumed to gain credit, and continued to ruin. Respecting *public* affairs, the difference is still greater. In England, the salaries of officers, and emoluments of office are enormous. The king has a million sterling per annum, and yet cannot maintain his family free of debt: secretaries of state, lords of treasury, admiralty, &c. have vast appointments: an auditor of the exchequer has sixpence in the pound, or a fortieth part of all the public money expended by the nation; so that when a war costs forty

millions one million is paid to him: an inspector of the mint, in the last new coinage, received as his fee 65,000*l.* sterling per annum; to all which rewards no service these gentlemen can render the public is by any means equivalent. All this is paid by the people, who are oppressed by taxes so occasioned, and thereby rendered less able to contribute to the payment of necessary national debts. In America, salaries, where indispensible, are extremely low; but much of the public business is done gratis. The honour of serving the public ably and faithfully is deemed sufficient. *Public spirit* really exists there, and has great effects. In England it is universally deemed a non-entity, and whoever pretends to it is laughed at as a fool, or suspected as a knave. The committees of congress which form the board of war, the board of treasury, the board of foreign affairs, the naval board, that for accounts, &c. all attend the business of their respective functions, without any salary or emolument whatever, though they spend in it much more of their time than any lord of treasury or admiralty in England can spare from his amusements. A British minister lately computed, that the whole expence of the Americans, in their *civil* government over three millions of people amounted to but 70,000*l.* sterling, and drew from thence a conclusion, that they ought to be taxed, until their expence was equal in proportion to that which it costs Britain to govern eight millions. He had no idea of a contrary conclusion, that if three millions may be well governed for 70,000*l.* eight millions may be as well governed for three times that sum, and that therefore the expence of his own government should be diminished. In that corrupted nation no man is ashamed of being concerned in lucrative *government jobs*, in which the public money is egregiously misapplied and squandered, the treasury pillaged, and more numerous and heavy taxes accumulated, to the great oppression of the people. But the prospect of a greater number of such jobs by a war is an inducement with many, to cry out for war upon all occasions, and to oppose every proposition of peace. Hence the constant increase of the national debt, and the absolute improbability of its ever being discharged.

4. Respecting the *amount and certainty of income, and solidity of security*; the *whole* thirteen states of America are engaged for the payment of every debt contracted by the congress, and the debt to be contracted by the present war is the *only* debt they will have to pay; all, or nearly all, the former debts of particular colonies being already discharged. Whereas England will have to pay not only the enormous debt this war must occasion, but all their vast preceding debt, or the interest of it,—and while America is enriching itself by prizes made upon the British commerce, more than it ever did by any commerce of its own, under the restraints of a British monopoly; Britain is growing poorer by the loss of that monopoly, and the diminution of its revenues, and of course less able to discharge the present indiscreet increase of its expences.

5. Respecting prospects of greater future ability, Britain has none such. Her islands are circumscribed by the ocean; and excepting a few parks or forests, she has no new land to cultivate, and cannot therefore extend her improvements. Her numbers too, instead of

increasing from increased subsistence, are continually diminishing from growing luxury, and the increasing difficulties of maintaining families, which of course discourage early marriages. Thus she will have fewer people to assist in paying her debts, and that diminished number will be poorer. America, on the contrary, has, besides her lands already cultivated, a vast territory yet to be cultivated; which, being cultivated, continually increases in value with the increase of people; and the people, who double themselves by a *natural propagation* every twenty-five years, will double yet faster, by the accession of *strangers*, as long as lands are to be had for new families; so that every twenty years there will be a double number of inhabitants obliged to discharge the public debts; and those inhabitants, being more opulent, may pay their shares with greater ease.

6. Respecting *prudence* in general affairs, and the advantages to be expected from the loan desired; the Americans are cultivators of land; those engaged in fishery and commerce are few, compared with the others. They have ever conducted their several governments with wisdom, avoiding wars, and vain expensive projects, delighting only in their peaceable occupations, which must, considering the extent of their uncultivated territory, find them employment still for ages. Whereas England, ever unquiet, ambitious, avaricious, imprudent, and quarrelsome, is half of the time engaged in war, always at an expence infinitely greater than the advantage to be obtained by it, if successful. Thus they made war against Spain in 1739, for a claim of about 95,000*l.* (scarce a groat for each

individual of the nation) and spent forty millions sterling in the war, and the lives of fifty thousand men; and finally made peace without obtaining satisfaction for the sum claimed. Indeed, there is scarce a nation in Europe, against which she has not made war on some frivolous pretext or other, and thereby imprudently accumulated a debt, that has brought her on the verge of bankruptcy. But the most indiscreet of all her wars, is the present against America, with whom she might, for ages, have preserved her profitable connection only by a just and equitable conduct. She is now acting like a mad shop-keeper, who, by beating those that pass his doors, attempts to make them come in and be his customers. America cannot submit to such treatment, without being first ruined, and, being ruined, her custom will be worth nothing. England, to effect this, is increasing her debt, and irretrievably ruining herself. America, on the other hand, aims only to establish her liberty, and that freedom of commerce which will be advantageous to all Europe; and by abolishing that monopoly which she laboured under, she will profit infinitely more than enough to repay any debt, which she may contract to accomplish it.

7. Respecting *character in the honest payment of debts*; the punctuality with which America has discharged her public debts was shown under the first head. And the general good disposition of the people to such punctuality has been manifested in their faithful payment of *private* debts to England, since the commencement of this war. There were not wanting some politicians [in America] who proposed *stopping that payment*, until peace should be restored, alleging,

that in the usual course of commerce, and of the credit given, there was always a debt existing equal to the trade of eighteen months: that the trade amounting to five millions sterling per annum, the debt must be seven millions and an half; that this sum paid to the British merchants would operate to prevent that distress, intended to be brought upon Britain, by our stoppage of commerce with her; for the merchants, receiving this money, and no orders with it for farther supplies, would either lay it out in the public funds, or in employing manufacturers to accumulate goods for a future hungry market in America upon an expected accommodation, by which means the funds would be kept up and the manufacturers prevented from murmuring. But *against this it was alleged*, that injuries from ministers should not be revenged on merchants; that the credit was in consequence of private contracts, made in confidence of good faith; that these ought to be held sacred and faithfully complied with; for that, whatever public utility might be supposed to arise from a breach of private faith, it was unjust, and would in the end be found unwise—honesty being in truth the best policy. On this principle the proposition was universally rejected; and though the English prosecuted the war with unexampled barbarity, burning our defenceless towns in the midst of winter, and arming savages against us; the debt was punctually paid; and the merchants of London have testified to the parliament, and will testify to all the world, that from their experience in dealing with us they had, before the war, no apprehension of our unfairness; and that since the war they have been convinced, that their good opinion of us was well founded. England, on the contrary, an old, corrupt, extravagant, and profligate nation, sees herself deep in debt, which she is in no condition to pay; and yet is madly, and dishonestly running deeper, without any possibility of discharging her debt, but by a public bankruptcy.

It appears, therefore, from the general industry, frugality, ability, prudence, and virtue of America, that she is a much safer debtor than Britain;—to say nothing of the satisfaction generous minds must have in reflecting, that by loans to America they are opposing tyranny, and aiding the cause of liberty, which is the cause of all mankind.

5.

Final Speech of Dr. Franklin at the Constitutional Convention

1787

MR. PRESIDENT,

I confess that I do not entirely approve of this constitution at present: but, Sir, I am not sure I shall never approve it; for having lived long, I have experienced many instances of being obliged, by better information, or fuller consideration, to change opinions, even on important subjects, which I once thought right, but found to be otherwise. It is, therefore, that, the older I grow, the more apt I am to doubt my own judgment, and to pay more respect to the judgment of others. Most men, indeed, as well as most sects in religion, think themselves in possession of all truth, and that whenever others differ from them, it is so far error. Steel, a protestant, in a dedication, tells the pope, that "the only difference between our two churches, in their opinions of the certainty of their doctrines is, the Romish church is infallible, and the church of England never in the wrong." But, though many private persons think almost as highly of their own infallibility as of that of their sect, few express it so naturally as a certain French lady, who, in a little dispute with her sister, said, I don't know how it happens, sister, but I meet with nobody but myself that is always in the right. *Il n'y a que moi qui a toujours raison.* In these sentiments, Sir, I agree to this constitution, with all its faults, if they are such, because I think a general government necessary for us, and there is no form of government but what may be a blessing, if well administered; and I believe farther, that this is likely to be well administered for a course of years, and can only end in despotism, as other forms have done before it, when the people shall become so corrupted as to need despotic government, being incapable of any other. I doubt too, whether any other convention we can obtain, may be able to make a better constitution. For when you assemble a number of men, to have the advantage of their joint wisdom, you inevitably assemble with those men, all their prejudices, their passions, their errors of opinion, their local interests, and their selfish views. From such an assembly can a perfect production be expected? It therefore astonishes me, sir, to find this system approaching so near to perfection as it does; and I think it will astonish our enemies, who are waiting with confidence to hear, that our councils are confounded, like those of the builders of Babylon, and that our states are on the point of separation, only to meet hereafter for the purpose of cutting each other's throats.

Thus I consent, sir, to this constitution, because I expect no better, and because I am not sure, that this is not the best. The opinions I have had of its errors, I sacrifice to the public good. I have never whispered a syllable of them abroad. Within these walls they were born, and here they shall die. If every one of us, in returning to our constituents, were to report the objections he has had to it, and endeavour to gain partisans in support of them, we might prevent its being generally received, and thereby lose all the salutary effects and great advantages resulting naturally in our favour among foreign nations, as well as among ourselves, from our real or apparent unanimity. Much of the strength and efficiency of any government, in procuring and securing happiness to the people, depends on opinion, on the general opinion of the goodness of that government, as well as of the wisdom and integrity of its governors.

I hope therefore, that for our own sakes, as part of the people, and for the sake of our posterity, we shall act heartily and unanimously in recommending this constitution, wherever our influence may extend, and turn our future thoughts and endeavours to the means of having it well administered.

On the whole, sir, I cannot help expressing a wish, that every member of the convention, who may still have objections, would with me, on this occasion, doubt a little of his own infallibility, and, to make manifest our unanimity, put his name to this instrument.

6.

An Address to the Public, from the Pennsylvania Society for Promoting the Abolition of Slavery

1789

It is with peculiar satisfaction, we assure the friends of humanity, that, in prosecuting the design of our association, our endeavours have proved successful, far beyond our most sanguine expectations.

Encouraged by this success, and by the daily progress of that luminous and benign spirit of liberty, which is diffusing itself throughout the world, and humbly hoping for the continuance of the divine blessing on our labours, we have ventured to make an important addition to our original plan, and do, therefore, earnestly solicit the support and assistance of all, who can feel the tender emotions of sympathy and compassion, or relish the exalted pleasure of beneficence.

Slavery is such an atrocious debasement of human nature, that its very extirpation, if not performed with solicitous care, may sometimes open a source of serious evils.

The unhappy man, who has long been treated as a brute animal, too frequently sinks beneath the common standard of the human species. The galling chains, that bind his body, do also fetter his intellectual faculties, and impair the social affections of his heart. Accustomed to move like a mere machine, by the will of a master, reflection is suspended; he has not the power of choice; and reason and conscience have but little influence over his conduct, because he is chiefly governed by the passion of fear. He is poor and friendless—perhaps worn out by extreme labour, age, and disease.

Under such circumstances, freedom may often prove a misfortune to himself, and prejudicial to society.

Attention to emancipated black people, it is therefore to be hoped, will become a branch of our national police; but as far as we contribute to promote this emancipation, so far that attention is evidently a serious duty incumbent on us, and which we mean to discharge to the best of our judgment and abilities.

To instruct, to advise, to qualify those, who have been restored to freedom, for the exercise and enjoyment of civil liberty, to promote in them habits of industry, to furnish them with employments suited to their age, sex, talents, and other circumstances, and to procure their children an education calculated for their future situation in life; these are the great outlines of the annexed plan, which we have adopted, and which we conceive will essentially promote the public good, and the happiness of these our hitherto too much neglected fellow-creatures.

A plan so extensive cannot be carried into execution without considerable pecuniary resources, beyond the present ordinary funds of the society. We hope much from the generosity of enlightened and benevolent freemen, and will gratefully receive any donations or subscriptions for this purpose, which may be made to our treasurer, James Starr, or to James Pemberton, chairman of our committee of correspondence.

Signed by order of the society,

B. FRANKLIN, PRESIDENT.

Philadelphia,
9th of November, 1789.

7.

Petition to Congress from the Pennsylvania Society for the Abolition of Slavery

1790

To the Senate & House of Representatives of the United States,
The Memorial of the Pennsylvania Society for promoting the Abolition of Slavery, the relief of free Negroes unlawfully held in bondage, & the Improvement of the Condition of the African Races. Respectfully Sheweth,

That from a regard for the happiness of Mankind an Association was formed several years since in this State by a number of her Citizens of various religious denominations for promoting the Abolition of Slavery & for the relief of those unlawfully held in bondage. A just & accurate Conception of the true Principles of liberty, as it spread through the land, produced accessions to their numbers, many friends to their

Cause, & a legislative Co-operation with their views, which, by the blessing of Divine Providence, have been successfully directed to the relieving from bondage a large number of their fellow Creatures of the African Race. They have also the Satisfaction to observe, that in consequence of that Spirit of Philanthropy & genuine liberty which is generally diffusing its beneficial Influence, similar Institutions are gradually forming at home & abroad.

That mankind are all formed by the same Almighty being, alike objects of his Care & equally designed for the Enjoyment of Happiness the Christian Religion teaches us to believe & the Political Creed of America fully coincides with the Position. Your Memorialists, particularly engaged in attending to the Distresses arising from Slavery, believe it their indispensable Duty to present this Subject to your notice. They have observed with great Satisfaction that many important & salutary Powers are vested in you for "promoting the Welfare & Securing the blessings of liberty to the "People of the United States." And as they conceive, that these blessings ought rightfully to be administered, without distinction of Colour, to all descriptions of People, so they indulge themselves in the pleasing expectation, that nothing, which can be done for the relive of the unhappy objects of their care, will be either omitted or delayed.

From a persuasion that equal liberty was originally the Portion, It is still the Birthright of all men, & influenced by the strong ties of Humanity & the Principles of their Institution, your Memorialists conceive themselves bound to use all justifiable endeavours to loosen the bounds of Slavery and promote a general Enjoyment of the blessings of Freedom. Under these Impressions they earnestly entreat your serious attention to the Subject of Slavery, that you will be pleased to countenance the Restoration of liberty to those unhappy Men, who alone, in this land of Freedom, are degraded into perpetual Bondage, and who, amidst the general Joy of surrounding Freemen, are groaning in Servile Subjection, that you will devise means for removing this Inconsistency from the Character of the American People, that you will promote mercy and Justice towards this distressed Race, & that you will Step to the very verge of the Powers vested in you for discouraging every Species of Traffick in the Persons of our fellow men.

Philadelphia, February 3, 1790
B. FRANKLIN
President of the Society

8.

Letter to the Editor
on the Slave Trade

1790

To the Editor of the *Federal Gazette*
March 23d, 1790.

Sir,
Reading last night in your excellent Paper the speech of
Mr. Jackson in Congress against their meddling with
the Affair of Slavery, or attempting to mend the
Condition of the Slaves, it put me in mind of a similar
One made about 100 Years since by Sidi Mehemet
Ibrahim, a member of the Divan of Algiers, which may
be seen in Martin's Account of his Consulship, anno
1687. It was against granting the Petition of the Sect
called *Erika*, or Purists who pray'd for the Abolition of
Piracy and Slavery as being unjust. Mr. Jackson does
not quote it; perhaps he has not seen it. If, therefore,
some of its Reasonings are to be found in his eloquent
Speech, it may only show that men's Interests and
Intellects operate and are operated on with surprising
similarity in all Countries and Climates, when under

similar Circumstances. The African's Speech, as translated, is as follows.

"Allah Bismillah, &c. God is great, and Mahomet is his Prophet.

"Have these *Erika* considered the Consequences of granting their Petition? If we cease our Cruises against the Christians, how shall we be furnished with the Commodities their Countries produce, and which are so necessary for us? If we forbear to make Slaves of their People, who in this hot Climate are to cultivate our Lands? Who are to perform the common Labours of our City, and in our Families? Must we not then be our own Slaves? And is there not more Compassion and more Favour due to us as Mussulmen, than to these Christian Dogs? We have now about 50,000 Slaves in and near Algiers. This Number, if not kept up by fresh Supplies, will soon diminish, and be gradually annihilated. If we then cease taking and plundering the Infidel Ships, and making Slaves of the Seamen and Passengers, our Lands will become of no Value for want of Cultivation; the Rents of Houses in the City will sink one half; and the Revenues of Government arising from its Share of Prizes be totally destroy'd! And for what? To gratify the whims of a whimsical Sect, who would have us, not only forbear making more Slaves, but even to manumit those we have.

"But who is to indemnify their Masters for the Loss? Will the State do it? Is our Treasury sufficient? Will the *Erika* do it? Can they do it? Or would they, to do what they think Justice to the Slaves, do a greater Injustice to the Owners? And it we set our Slaves free, what is to be done with them? Few of them will return to their Countries; they know too well the great Hardships they must there be subject to; they will not embrace our holy Religion; they will not adopt our Manners; our People will not pollute themselves by intermarrying with them. Must we maintain them as Beggars in our Streets, or suffer our Properties to be the Prey of their Pillage? For men long accustom'd to Slavery will not work for a Livelihood when not compell'd. And what is there so pitiable in their present Condition? Were they not Slaves in their own Countries?

"Are not Spain, Portugal, France, and the Italian states govern'd by Despots, who hold all their Subjects in Slavery, without Exception? Even England treats its Sailors as Slaves; for they are, whenever the Government pleases, seiz'd, and confin'd in Ships of War, condemn'd not only to work, but to fight, for small Wages, or a mere Subsistence, not better than our Slaves are allow'd by us. Is their Condition then made worse by their falling into our Hands? No; they have only exchanged on Slavery for another, and I may say a better; for here they are brought into a land where the Sun of Islamism gives forth its Light, and shines in full Splendor, and they have an Opportunity of making themselves acquainted with the true Doctrine, and thereby saving their immortal Souls. Those who remain at home have not that Happiness. Sending the Slaves home then would be sending them out of Light into Darkness.

"I repeat the Question, What is to be done with them? I have heard it suggested, that they may be planted in the Wilderness, where there is plenty of Land for them to subsist on, and where they may flourish as a free State; but they are, I doubt, to little dispos'd to labour without Compulsion, as well as too ignorant to establish a good government, and the wild Arabs would soon molest and destroy or again enslave them. While serving us, we take care to provide them with every thing, and they are treated with Humanity. The Labourers in their own Country are, as I am well informed, worse fed, lodged, and cloathed. The Condition of most of them is therefore already mended, and requires no further Improvement. Here their Lives are in Safety. They are not liable to be impress'd for Soldiers, and forc'd to cut one another's Christian throats, as in the Wars of their own Countries. If some of the religious mad Bigots, who now teaze us with their silly Petitions, have in a Fit of blind Zeal freed their Slaves, it was not Generosity, it was not Humanity, that mov'd them to the Action; it was from the conscious Burthen of a Load of Sins, and Hope, from the supposed Merits of so good a Work, to be excus'd Damnation.

"How grossly are they mistaken in imagining Slavery to be disallow'd by the Alcoran? Are not the two Precepts, to quote no more, *Masters, treat your Slaves with kindness; Slaves, serve your Masters with Cheerfulness and Fidelity,*' clear Proofs to the contrary? Nor can the Plundering of Infidels be in that sacred Book forbidden, since it is well known from it, that God has given the World, and all that it contains, to his faithful Mussulmen, who are to enjoy it of Right as fast as they conquer it. Let us then hear no more of this detestable Proposition, the Manumission of Christian Slaves, the Adoption of which would, by depreciating our Lands and Houses, and thereby depriving so many good Citizens of their Properties, create universal Discontent, and provoke Insurrections, to the endangering of Government and producing general Confusion. I have therefore no doubt, but this wise Council will prefer the Comfort and Happiness of a whole Nation of true Believers to the Whim of a few *Erika*, and dismiss their Petition."

The Result was, as Martin tells us, that the Divan came to this Resolution; "The Doctrine, that Plundering and Enslaving the Christians is unjust, is at best *problematical*; but that it is the Interest of this State to continue the Practice, is clear; therefore let the Petition be rejected."

And it was rejected accordingly.

And since like Motives are apt to produce in the Minds of Men like Opinions and Resolutions, may we not, Mr. Brown, venture to predict, from this Account, that the Petitions to the Parliament of England for abolishing the Slave-Trade, to say nothing of other Legislatures, and the Debates upon them, will have a similar Conclusion?

I am, Sir, your constant Reader and humble Servant,

HISTORICUS.

ABOUT THE PUBLISHER

Corpus Editing is a small, independent publisher of books on United States history, American culture, and English as a Second Language.

We publish original materials and academic texts, as well as documents and literature in the public domain that form an integral part of the American experience.

Corpus Editing publishes works such as those of Benjamin Franklin reproduced here in hopes that these important ideas will continue to reach a modern audience.

Inquiries may be directed to miller@fwu.ac.jp